TEDDY BEARS AND DOODLEBUGS

TEDDY BEARS AND DOODLEBUGS

A London Child's View of World War Two

Jacqueline Hollings

Book Guild Publishing
Sussex, England

First published in Great Britain in 2010 by
The Book Guild Ltd
Pavilion View
19 New Road
Brighton, BN1 1UF

Typesetting in Garamond by
YHT Ltd, London

Printed in Great Britain by
CPI Antony Rowe

A catalogue record for this book is available from
The British Library.

ISBN 978 1 84624 452 0

Dedicated to the memory of
ROSE, STANLEY and DOROTHY

Contents

Preface

We were watching television when my youngest son suddenly asked me what it was like in the war. I was initially stumped for an answer; it seemed so long ago. Those anxious times had long disappeared into the deepest recesses of my mind. Matters of career, marriage and family have occupied me since, almost eradicating all thought of those dark, fearful days of my childhood.

His question had been prompted by media coverage at the end of the 1980s, which marked the 50th anniversary of the outbreak of war in 1939. As we watched the story unfold on the screen, my memory gradually awakened and a kaleidoscopic jumble of incidents, images, sounds and emotions from the past began to sharpen into focus with increasing clarity. All sorts of details surfaced of life under conditions of war. But before I could provide an answer that would satisfy, a little research was necessary to make sense of all these snippets of imagery, to slot them properly into the context of the war's progress and to portray successfully an accurate picture of life for one typical family trying to deal with the routine of each day under such traumatic conditions.

From films, television documentaries, film archives, war diaries and autobiographies, we all know of the war's major events – Dunkirk, Pearl Harbor, the Blitz, the Battle of Britain, the Holocaust and the Normandy landings, and of its great leaders and heroes. But what of the civilians at home? How did they all cope? How did it affect the children?

Although less dramatic, the account that follows is another facet of that same epic. It is one that could also perhaps take its place among the records of such a momentous period in our history. Not the great battles, dramas, heroics, victories and defeats being played out abroad, but how those events influenced and touched the life of an ordinary little girl growing up amid the upheaval of those times.

So, for my son who raised the question that started my mind coursing back to reflect and ponder on a bewildering and stressful episode in my youth, for others who may also be curious (and with the possibility of my grandchildren one day making a similar enquiry), here is the story of our family's involvement in the drama of those six epoch-making years, written and recorded as one grandma remembers, seventy years on, before the details are forgotten and lost forever.

1

Getting Ready

As I was only eight years old when war began I had very little notion of what it was about. I had no understanding of the significance of the extraordinary events happening in the world, and no conception of the explosion of social values about to take place. I had no idea why we were fighting another war so soon after the previous one. Whenever the subject was raised adults spoke in hushed tones and refrained from discussing the darker issues when children were within earshot. So we remained ignorant for some time of the implications and political issues involved.

Explanations for the mysterious goings-on in the streets and parks, the diggings, the accumulation of sandbags, and sticky stuff covering windows were at first brief and vague: 'In case war comes'. Detailed explanations came later. I had no idea who Hitler was or why he was so evil. A child accepts and lives each day as it comes, trusting the adults around him, giving little thought to the future. But I could sense that everyone was fearful, so I was affected by the atmosphere of gloom surrounding us all.

We lived on a newish housing estate in north-west London within a few stones' throw of Hendon Aerodrome.

Dad worked for the *Daily Mail* in Blackfriars, central London, but at home he was gardener, musician, carpenter, photographer and breeder of budgerigars. Mum had been a ballet dancer but her three youngsters now kept her busily occupied, her dancing but a fast-fading memory. My sister Bronia aged seven and my brother Michael aged four completed the family.

Maternal grandmother Nanna Rose and paternal grandfather Grandpa Phil with their grandchildren Michael, Jacqueline and Bronia on a family day out in 1935.

Our lives pre-war were carefree. I have vague memories of day trips to Margate, holidays at Eastbourne and a holiday camp on Hayling Island. Children enjoyed much more freedom than they do now. Bronia, Michael and I spent a lot of time wandering about and playing with friends in our neighbourhood, exploring woodland and fields nearby, and picking wild blackberries. The Silk Stream, a meandering brook, was heaven. We loved to jump across it via slippery stepping-stones, and search for dabs with our fishing nets. We took them home in jars of water but I cannot recall their eventual fate. We were often stung by nettles but learned to soothe the stings with dock leaves. During our blissful days in the sunshine we were slow to notice the developing political storm or the clouds of doom which were gradually descending upon the adults around us.

Even before war began people must have been fairly sure it was coming for there was evidence all around us of preparation and protection. The huge piles of sandbags propped against public buildings were to protect them from bomb blast. Strips of sticky tape were stuck in patterns on windows to prevent splinters of glass causing injury after an explosion. Tube trains and buses had their windows almost covered by closely woven net, leaving only a small diamond-shaped space in the middle for passengers to peer out. Every station had its identifying name-signs blacked out so that enemy spies could not find out where they were. For the same reason all signposts were removed from street corners.

It was thought necessary to have a complete blackout of London and elsewhere after the war started. All lights were to be turned out so German aircraft crews would be unable to target our cities accurately. Practice blackouts were held beforehand. My mother bought some strong black material recommended for the purpose and hung some at each window of the house. No crack of light was to be seen from outside. If there was the smallest chink of light showing we soon had a knock and shout from a passing policeman or Air Raid Warden.

Kerbs were painted white at intervals, and white dotted lines appeared along the centres of roads to help both pedestrians and drivers. It was very dark and eerie after nightfall and everyone had to carry a torch, but we were discouraged from venturing forth at night.

Newspapers and radio broadcasts were peppered with the puzzling word 'war' but nobody explained to me what it meant. It was obvious that everyone was dreading it so, when Dad told us on Sunday morning 3rd September 1939 that there was to be an important announcement on the radio at 11.15 a.m., I felt a sense of foreboding without understanding the reason why.

We gathered around the wireless, as we then called it, to listen. The official declaration of war against Germany that morning was immediately followed by a spine-chilling wailing siren, which added to my fear. We had a neighbour with us at the time whose immediate reaction was to run home as fast as he could, which was quite comical. As always in times of crisis, Mum's reaction was to make a cup of tea. I followed her into the kitchen to toss a hundred questions at her. What *is* a war? What is going to happen? What was that wail? What does it all mean? I was told years later that my little face was as white as chalk and my whole body visibly shaking.

Dad spent the rest of the day continuing to dig a huge hole at the end of our small garden. He explained that an Anderson shelter was to be erected in the hole so that we could sleep in it and be safe from any bombs that Hitler's planes may drop. 'Who is Hitler?' I asked. 'He is a nasty, evil man in Germany who plans to conquer the whole world, so we have to stop him. He pretends to be friendly

4

but events have shown he cannot be trusted. We think that he is preparing to invade our country, but we cannot allow him to do so. If he succeeds we shall all lose our freedom.'

* * *

The garden was Dad's pride and joy. Along the back fence was an aviary he had designed and built himself, containing about thirty budgerigars. Its design, and the way it was incorporated into the garden's layout of rockeries, circular flowerbeds, a fish pond and lawns, had won third prize in a competition organised by the Cage Birds Annual. This was no small achievement considering the tiny size of the garden. As he dug, his heart must have been heavy, not only because of the war, but because he was having to dismantle the rockery and fish pond and replace them with

Our back garden in Colindale, showing the aviary Dad built for the budgerigars in 1936. The Anderson shelter was later erected under the rockery by the back fence.

a shelter made of ugly corrugated metal. But, typical of his ingenuity and imagination, he managed to organise things so that the rockery could be rebuilt to continue up and over the shelter. When all was finished we could not see it from the house. The entrance was cleverly concealed, positioned at right angles to the back fence. The following spring the shelter was hidden under a mass of mauve and yellow flowers.

Inside it, he built a pair of bunk beds along one side for my sister and me, a small bed along the opposite side for my brother, and into the remaining space he somehow managed to squeeze a bed just large enough for Mum and himself. A curtain, made from an old thinning blanket, was used to draw across the beds for privacy. There was also a shelf where matches, candles and a torch were kept. The door had a little square peep-hole which could be opened by sliding its cover sideways.

Beyond the back fence was a large, rough unused field backed by houses on three sides. Dad had earlier cut a gate into the fence to form a back entrance enabling us to take a short cut through the field to the buses and the Underground tube station. When we first began to use the shelter in the days before Hitler started bombing us, we children would lie on our bunks listening for Dad to return from work. As soon as we heard the fence gate creak we all shouted 'Goodnight!' and he would slide open the peep-hole in the door to reply. Sometimes he came into the shelter to tuck us up and have a little chat before joining Mum in the house.

* * *

There was yet more digging to be done. Posters everywhere instructed us to 'Dig for Victory'. The field behind us was carved up into strips of allotments and used by the residents whose gardens backed onto it. Our allotment was alongside the back fence, bordered by a path which led from the gate. Dad spent much of the autumn of 1939 digging, planting and sowing his patch with assorted seeds and vegetables in neat rows. We were lucky to have use of the field and so not have to spoil more of our garden.

All metal objects that could be spared were called in for scrap to help build aeroplanes, guns and ammunition. I recall a horse-drawn cart wending its way around our little cul-de-sac, the collector calling out for any spare metal. Mum gave him some items, as did some of our neighbours.

The metal railings that had surrounded the bed of laurel bushes in the centre of the road were dismantled. That was good news for the children. Henceforth we could dive into and through the bushes to reach our friends and homes on the other side – much more fun than walking around! We played games, built camps, hatched plots and made plans among those bushes. They became a main centre of play during our childhood.

* * *

A large brick shelter was built at the entrance to our road. Perhaps it was reinforced in some way but at the time I could not see the point of it, wondering how it could be any more safe than the houses nearby. Our family never used it, but while it was being erected local children played Houses, Battles and Camps inside it in the evenings after the builders had left and at weekends. We rearranged all the loose bricks to make walls and sorted ourselves into friends and foes, English and German or cowboys and indians, 'firing' at each other from opposite ends and taking refuge behind our own walls.

I soon found that its outside walls were marvellous for playing ball games. After school I played hours of 'Dropsy' and 'Double Dropsy' with a ball against the wall. When my two friends and I had perfected our skills we progressed to throwing two balls at the same time. I never reached the dizzy heights of juggling with three balls as my friend did, but I watched her do so with a mixture of awe, envy and admiration.

Skipping, hoop-rolling, hopscotch and top-spinning were other favourite pastimes. I was once able to keep my little wooden top spinning all the way to school with the help of a stick and string – but only once. It was fun to find who could keep the top spinning for the longest time.

* * *

Every man, woman and child in the country was issued with a gas mask. There was a real fear that Hitler would be nasty enough to use gas as a weapon. Gas masks were unpleasant to wear, smelled strongly of rubber, fitted tightly around our faces and were claustrophobic. We never noticed that Mum, who suffered from asthma, managed to avoid putting hers on but she insisted that we became used to wearing ours. She regularly held a gas-mask drill. As soon as we heard her ringing the little bell, we had to stop whatever we were doing to see how quickly we could get the masks on and properly fixed. We never enjoyed this, but complied reluctantly.

Wooden poles supporting flat, square pieces of wood began to appear at roadsides. It was explained that if the surface turned green it would indicate that poison gas was in the air and we were immediately to put on our gas masks.

Tiny babies had special masks into which they could be

8

inserted and zipped. Infants under two years old had masks that covered their heads and chests. These were decorated with pictures of Mickey Mouse but that did not prevent many children from kicking and screaming against being placed into them.

Nobody was allowed out without carrying a gas mask. Each was kept in a square cardboard box and hung over the shoulder by a long strap. They were often subject to misuse and careless treatment so had to be regularly tested. When we had visitors, or when we were visiting relatives and friends, we had to check that everyone had his mask before leaving. It became common to chant a silly rhyme at the door when saying goodbye.

'Got yer gas mask?
Got yer torchlight?
All right?
Goodnight!'

Invariably followed by laughter.

Hitler never used gas against us during the war – but we weren't to know that at the time and had to be prepared.

* * *

The Government asked all able-bodied women to become ambulance drivers, join the Women's Voluntary Service (WVS), work in factories, help farmers by joining the Land Army, train as auxiliary nurses, Red Cross workers etc., or enlist in the Armed Forces.

Those with young children were exempt from other work but Mum wanted to Do Something, so she appealed to the headmaster of the local infant school to include Michael among the new intake, although he would not be five until early November. At first he said 'No, rules are rules', but he later wrote to Mum saying he could not forget the forlorn look on her face, so he was prepared to make an exception in Michael's case. She was delighted as it meant she was now free to do her bit for the war effort.

At first she tried part-time work in a factory but that did not last long (perhaps because of her asthma). Later, she joined the Hendon Food Office helping with the issue of ration books to everyone in the Borough of Hendon. She enjoyed this, made new friends, and found there were perks such as having access to everyone's records and discovering the ages of all our neighbours! She never let on, of course, but it amused her to be in possession of their secrets. Somehow she always managed to be home before we returned from school and during school holidays.

* * *

After the initial fright and panic caused by the siren that followed Neville Chamberlain's broadcast on 3rd September (the siren had been a false alarm) all became strangely quiet at the lack of news concerning the war's progress. Life continued much as normal, with everyone going about their usual routine tasks, attending school, going to work and, in my case, daily piano practice. The war seemed unreal and far away, although I noticed trenches being dug in local parks and open spaces, mounds of earth left between, and poles and stakes pierced into the ground (to prevent landing of enemy planes I was told).

Cinemas and theatres had closed but gradually opened again. There were announcements about petrol rationing, what to do if an air-raid Alert sounded, how to obtain one's ration book, and where young men were to report for enlisting into the Army, Navy or Air Force.

The sky became filled with hundreds of floating silver

barrage balloons (to stop the enemy flying too low) and the dark blacked-out evenings ensured that most of us stayed indoors after then.

The country settled down into a sort of restive calm, going about its daily business wondering, watching and waiting...

Bronia, Jacqueline and Michael in 1939.

2

What Now?

The atmosphere of quiet unease at home continued into the autumn, through winter and into spring. News began to filter through of German U-boats prowling the Atlantic and successfully attacking our shipping. Hitler's armies continued to overrun Europe, and Poland surrendered. In April, the Germans invaded Norway.

All fit men under the age of twenty-three were called up into the Armed Forces and reported for their medicals. Food gradually became more scarce and ration books were issued to everybody to ensure fair distribution of food. Each page of the book was given a label such as meat, cheese, bacon, sugar or butter, etc. and was divided into coupons, which shopkeepers either crossed or cut out whenever a purchase was made.

Anyone could be stopped at any time to have his identity checked, so it was essential for us all to carry an identity card and number. During the first few months of the war while all was still quiet on the home front - a period known as the 'Phoney War' - visits between family and friends continued much as before, but visitors always took food with them for their hosts, i.e. butter, sugar or tea, as rationing severely restricted the amount available.

Although we lived in north London, most of our relatives lived south of the Thames in Thornton Heath, Norwood, New Malden and Thames Ditton. We continued to make journeys across London to see them, especially my maternal grandmother, known to us as Nanna. She and Grandpa lived in Thornton Heath and our trips across the City by tube train and bus remained without incident for some months, but once the Blitz brought the war to our very doorstep all non-essential journeys were stopped. Posters went up everywhere asking 'Is Your Journey Really Necessary?', making us feel a trifle guilty when travelling about.

A policeman checks identification labels and gives a helping hand to evacuees leaving London for places of safety during 1939 and 1940. (© Imperial War Museum LN6194).

* * *

14

Christmas always arrived for us the moment Nanna entered the house. She and Grandpa arrived two days before Christmas Day carrying suitcases, and bags bulging with mysterious parcels. Nanna took a childlike delight in the festivities, never losing a child's wonder, awe and happiness of the occasion. She was not the sort to allow the inconvenience and austerity of war to spoil the family fun and fully entered into the spirit of things as ever.

I cannot recall a Christmas without a tree but where my parents obtained one during wartime I have no idea. There it was, resplendent with lights and tinsel as usual in the corner of the lounge when we came down to breakfast on Christmas morning. We never saw a hint of decorations until that moment, so Christmas Day held a special magic for us. Mum and Dad must have worked like demons the previous evening to make sure all was ready by morning. Presents surrounded the tree, but we were not to open any until after dinner was over and the kitchen tidy.

On Christmas morning I caught Nanna bending secretively over the parcels enjoying a sneaky read of the labels. At my shout of 'Nanna!' she guiltily jumped aside, laughed, and said she was just checking to see if they were all there!

At Christmas the small kitchen was out of bounds to everyone except the two cooks. However, curious at hearing strange noises coming from within, I opened the door to find both Mum and Nanna doubled up with hilarity and hunched over a messy splosh of food splattered about the floor with the half-roasted chicken. They were both rocking with helpless uncontrolled laughter as they scooped up the greasy mess, rescuing as much as they could and replacing it in the roasting tin. One of them had taken the tin out of the oven to baste the chicken and vegetables, then dropped the lot. As she spooned it back

Nanna spluttered through her chuckles, 'What the eye don't see, the heart won't grieve over', and Mum added to me, 'Don't you dare tell the others'.

Our family enjoyed their Christmas dinner as much as ever that year, the cooks still quietly giggling. Nanna's looks and behaviour belied her age by about twenty years. She and Mum were great pals and we all loved her dearly.

* * *

The winter of 1939–40 was exceedingly cold and bleak, with deep snow lying on the ground for weeks. Supplies of coal nearly ran out resulting in sudden and frequent power cuts. A supply of candles had to be kept at the ready, and our little Valor stove was often in use as an alternative method of cooking and heating. Outside the ironmonger's were queues of people clutching cans whenever it was rumoured that a fresh supply of paraffin was in stock, and I was often sent out to buy some.

We were all asked to conserve energy, turning out lights that were not in use, using only six inches of water in our baths and lighting only one fire in the house. In those pre-central-heating days the family sat huddled around the living-room fire or paraffin stove. Mum did as much cooking as possible on the open fire and we often sat in front of it toasting bread at the end of long-handled toasting forks. Dripping on toast was a supper favourite.

Neighbours helped each other in many ways. They shared each others' ovens, each one taking her turn at cooking friends' dinners.

There was ice and frost on the windows at night; downstairs and up, inside and out. Bedrooms were always freezing and we wore our dressing-gowns in bed. Mum rolled us in flannelette sheets before tucking us under blankets and eiderdowns. It took at least half an hour before we were warm enough to sleep.

Each day began with Mum on her knees raking out the cold ashes from the fire of the previous day, her hands blue with cold. After the hearth was cleaned she placed scrunched-up balls of newspaper under fresh pieces of coal or wood before applying a lighted match. A large sheet of newspaper was held against the surround to act as bellows to draw up the flames. With the fire burning brightly and the chill off the living room we were called down to breakfast, usually a saucepan of porridge simmering on the stove in the middle of the room. Before we braved the snow in the twenty-minute walk to school, Mum warmed our socks, scarves, mittens and pixie-hoods on the stove so that we would have a warm start.

But before long the tops of my wellington boots were chafing around my legs causing sore red rings, and my hands were stiff and frozen. I suffered badly from chilblains so my toes were itchy and painful all day at school, and walking became difficult. One time they were so bad I stayed home for two days. On the second day I opened the door to the school's attendance officer who demanded to know why I was not at school. When I explained about the chilblains he said if I could walk to the door I could walk to school, and to see that I did so next day. Nanna made me a pair of leather spats with fur-fabric trim to wear over my shoes to keep my feet warm. They weren't very popular with me because other children did not wear anything like it and I hated to be different. When I was finally persuaded to wear them they proved fairly effective, but it was many years before the chilblain problem was solved.

Piano practice was a problem during winter because the lounge was always so cold. If there was insufficient fuel to allow the luxury of a second fire I wrapped a blanket around my thighs and legs, wore several thick old woollies, rested my feet on a rubber hot water bottle, had another on my lap, and gradually increased the blood-flow through my fingers by playing scales up and down the length of the keyboard. It took ages before I stopped shivering but eventually I was glowing with warmth, and my fingers were relaxed and supple enough to tackle the music.

One day, Dad arrived home early to find me cluttered up inside blankets and woollies at the piano. I was fearful of his reaction because he believed in Being Tough and not letting minor inconveniences such as freezing cold get in the way of One's Duty. To my surprise he was really pleased. 'That's what I like to see - using your initiative to counter difficulties, and not using the cold as an excuse for not practising.'

* * *

After rising one bitter February morning we discovered that all the budgerigars in the aviary had frozen to death. I had never known my parents so upset. One bird had been brought into the house when very young and lived in a cage in the living room. We called him Boysie and he developed a lovable, cheeky personality, was a friendly little character and a constant chatterbox. He taught himself to imitate the sounds around him.

Visitors were startled to hear him call out clearly and quickly in his shrill, repetitive, staccato tones, 'You naughty children - hello Boysie - hello - stop it - stop it at once - Jacqueline, Bronia, Michael - hello - do you hear me?' - on and on and on. He paced up and down in his cage by the door when he wanted to be let out (we called it The Lambeth Walk) and every day we allowed him out for a while to fly around, eat with us off the table and perch on our heads. Boysie was one of the family, giving us hours of pleasure at a down time in our lives.

Burst pipes and flooding became a common occurrence during that hard winter, adding to the many difficulties and general misery. Colds were frequent and severe. Mum's favourite remedy was to lie us on the floor in a row in front of the fire and rub some Vick into our chests.

* * *

Another change in our garden came the day Dad decided to adapt the aviary into a chicken coop, to supplement both meat and egg rations for the family. Inside the enclosure at one end he built a box in which he laid some straw, leaving a small entrance in one side for the chickens to come and go. At the top of the box he carefully positioned a notice, painting on it in black letters, 'Please Lay Eggs Here' with an arrow pointing to the entrance beneath. Michael amused us by reminding Dad that chickens cannot read! Nevertheless the hens obeyed the notice and kept us supplied in eggs, laid in the right place, for most of the war.

Owning chickens brought its problems, not least of which were rats. My parents acquired an airgun but were not skilled enough to shoot many, and the menace remained.

Every now and then, especially at Christmas, a chicken was killed for eating. Neither Mum nor Dad wanted to carry out the execution so a neighbour's help was sought. We looked the other way as the hen's neck was rung. Sometimes a hen stubbornly clung to life, so the job had to be finished with a hatchet. I shall never forget the moment one hen ran around the garden headless. We were told it had something to do with its nerves suffering shock reaction. I have never eaten chicken since without recalling that incident and feeling guilty because I did not become a vegetarian on the spot.

There was often a smell of boiling vegetation, peelings and food refuse emanating from the kitchen. It was an awful stench, which I can still recall. Some of it was for feeding the chickens but most became pigswill and was tipped into a bin, collected and passed on to farmers for their pigs. Pig farming was part of the Government's campaign for Britain to feed its own citizens as far as possible, imports by sea having been interrupted by the German navy. Hitler was claiming that his ships were successfully strangling Britain into submission, but this was a lie put out by his propaganda minister, 'Doctor' Goebbels.

A sentry standing guard on a south coast beach.
(© Imperial War Museum H4610).

* * *

20

My reports from school were usually good, so when one of them included the comment, 'does not concentrate in History', it caused enough concern for Dad to take me aside for a serious chat. I sat on his lap, swinging my legs against the sideboard while we studied together all the teacher's remarks.

I asked him what 'concentrate' means. He said it was what I was *not* doing at that moment. I was too busy swinging my legs and trying to tuck my toes under the sideboard's protruding drawer handles to pay much attention to what he was saying.

So what is history? This was our next topic. 'It is the story of lives long ago, of each person's contribution to man's progress and development, the growth of nations, scientific knowledge, laws, inventions. The reasons behind why we do this and that, what and how we think, the way we behave,' explained my father.

Like all children I found it almost impossible to comprehend the fact of anything existing before I was born. History lessons at school were boring stories of unreal people who had no relevance to, or influence upon, our own lives. But Dad pointed out that history never stops, it is a continuous story. It is *now*.

'We should learn how things were long ago so we can understand life today and work towards a better future. We are fighting a war because of past mistakes. We must learn from those mistakes and never repeat them.' He added that my grandchildren and great-grandchildren would one day read about Hitler, Churchill and the war in their history books.

Here was a new concept for me. History is *now*? From then on I perceived history in new light. After music, history became my favourite subject and I had no further trouble.

21

* * *

Rationing for a few items of food began in January 1940. We were allowed 4 oz ham, 4 oz bacon, 4 oz butter and 8 oz sugar each week. Meat was becoming scarce and was rationed later, the limit being approximately 1lb per week. There were no bananas, few oranges and not many sweets. I am convinced that Michael owes his exceptionally strong healthy teeth to the absence of sweets during his early childhood. Our diet consisted basically of the aptly named and dreaded tripe, which I loathed: rabbit, sausages and Spam. In her cooking, Mum used reconstituted eggs, which were in the form of a dark yellow powder. It was useful but not very popular. Occasionally we had whale meat; the taste of which was not unlike rabbit.

Mum was often short of money. When she couldn't afford to feed us she sent us to the British Restaurant in the High Street, where we were given a basic meal for six-pence each. Outside the restaurant was a huge circular water tank. It provided water for fighting fires caused by incendiary bombs. As it wasn't needed for some time, the surface became covered in green slime and exuded an unpleasant smell.

* * *

At the beginning of the war all able-bodied young men, other than those in vital services, e.g. food distribution, farming and the manufacture of weapons, were enlisted into the Armed Services. This was achieved according to age groups, the youngest going first. By the end of 1939 all the 18-21 year olds who had passed their medicals, had joined the Army, Navy or Air Force. During the first months of 1940 the 21-28 year-old age groups were called up in stages.

As Dad was thirty-one when war began he had a few months to go before his call-up papers were due. While waiting, he decided to join the Local Defence Volunteers, later known as the Home Guard. An appeal had gone out for men between the ages of 18–65, not in the Forces for various reasons, to provide an army at home for those who wished to help defend their country if invaded. These men were often teased for being amateurs. It was forgotten that the majority of the older men were veterans of the Great War twenty years earlier and the Boer War at the turn of the century. We became used to Dad in khaki uniform, and his rifle standing sentinel in the hall with the strictest of instructions never, *never* to touch or go anywhere near it.

The dreaded day arrived when Dad's enlisting papers came and he had to report for a medical. Over dinner soon afterwards he suddenly asked, 'How would you like to see me in Navy uniform?' Having introduced us to the news of his impending departure, he enlightened us further. It was actually, he said, a branch of the Navy known as The Royal Marines, and explained that a Marine was a combination of soldier and sailor with something of the skills and training of both. He thus gave us the impression that a Royal Marine was someone extra special. In our ignorance of war, as is the way with children, we felt pride and excitement – sentiments not shared by Mum and Dad who must have had totally different concerns and feelings as they finished their meal in a quiet and subdued mood.

* * *

Dad had given me my first piano lesson when I was four, and had coached me daily very successfully until about Grade 5 standard. But now that his call-up was imminent he had to make other arrangements for my musical training. He took me to the Guildhall School of Music and Drama in Blackfriars, central London, for an audition, and applied to Hendon Education Authority for a grant to cover the fees. We were all relieved and pleased when I passed the former and was allowed the latter, and my many years happy association with 'the Guildhall' began.

I travelled regularly on the Northern Line of the Underground into central London for a piano lesson every Saturday morning. By this time all station names were obliterated and train windows were covered with sticky mesh to minimize the effect of bomb blast. Not being able to see out easily to find where I was, I soon learned to recognise every nuance of sound along the line, memorising overground tunnel and bridge positions, the distances between each stop, and which side of the train the platform was situated at each station. I knew, for example, that when my ears popped I was under Hampstead Heath, between Golders Green and Hampstead stations.

Leaving the two younger children with a friend, Mum took me for the first three Saturdays, making sure I learned the way and how to change at Charing Cross for the Metropolitan Line. After that I was on my own – every Saturday morning during term time right through the war and afterwards until I was sixteen, when a change of teacher meant a switch to Thursday afternoons. At eighteen I became a full-time music student. Mum must have been quite frightened for me and very relieved each time I returned safely, especially as these journeys coincided with the start of air-raids and bombs, and I was still only nine.

* * *

Throughout the spring and summer of 1940 there was a lot of digging at the far end of the school field. I watched the men at work from the classroom window wondering what they were building. First they dug a row of long deep trenches, which were laid with concrete to make solid floors. Corrugated metal sheets were erected at the sides and over the top to form a round roof over each. They looked like rows of giant tunnels. Earth was thrown over the roofs so that, when finished, all I could see were rows of long mounds covered by freshly growing grass with a door at the end of each. We discovered all too soon what they were for as the new autumn term got under way.

* * *

News of the war was very discouraging that spring and summer. Hitler's troops had overrun Denmark, Norway, Belgium, Luxembourg and Holland. In June they had reached Paris and nobody seemed able to stop the Nazi menace. The British Army was trapped in France at Dunkirk, and was rescued from the beaches by a flotilla of small boats from England, but a lot of men were lost. The British also had to be evacuated from Norway.

There was a very real fear of invasion, for German troops were now only just across the Channel and must surely be poised for attack. The feelings of doom and dread were strong because we were now fighting Hitler on our own.

Our Government seemed ineffectual so there was a huge sense of relief when Neville Chamberlain resigned and Winston Churchill became Prime Minister of a National Coalition Government. Immediately there was a change of mood in the country. Churchill's gift of oratory was such that his speeches were very inspirational, and we listened to him on the radio as he stirred us all to greater effort,

Sir Winston Churchill at his seat in the Cabinet Room at No 10 Downing Street, London. (© Imperial War Museum MH26392)

increasing the people's courage, fortitude and their determination not to give in. We were all to stand up and fight for freedom against tyranny. He promised us blood, toil, tears and sweat before we achieved victory. He introduced the 'V for Victory' sign with the first two fingers of his right hand, using it as a salute wherever he went. Everyone adored him.

* * *

The Red Cross first aid, ambulance and rescue services, Civil Defence and WVS were gradually getting organised so that they would all be ready to spring into action with an immediate response in the event of an air raid with its inevitable casualties. They needed to rehearse their planned procedures to ensure maximum efficiency. One of their practices was held locally with the cooperation of our school, and they asked for as many children as possible to pretend to be refugees, wounded, homeless or lost – and wait for 'rescue'.

Thinking this would be a fun and welcome diversion from normal routine Bronia, Michael and I joined in. For a while we patiently endured having labels pinned to our chests with our names, addresses and details of pretend injuries, constantly being bandaged and re-bandaged, carried on stretchers here and there, herded into vans (which proved too much for Bronia. She thought she was being kidnapped and ran home screaming); and generally being shunted about aimlessly.

I never knew if the exercise was considered a success, but to me it all seemed a shambles. Michael and I eventually found our way home bewildered, thirsty, hungry and exhausted, not quite fully understanding what it was all about.

* * *

The plans to evacuate children from London and other big cities into the country and places of safety at the outbreak of war did not affect our family but, unknown to us, Mum and Dad had been quietly making alternative arrangements. These were so momentous that they kept their plans secret until almost the last moment, breaking it to us as gently and gradually as they could.

The first clues that something was afoot came when we were taken to the local welfare clinic for inoculations and vaccinations. There were many children lined up waiting their turn and we became increasingly apprehensive as the queue of children in front of us got smaller and some of them screamed in panic at the sight of the needle. We decided to be brave and Michael and I braced ourselves successfully for the prick, but Bronia faltered and shed a few tears.

The clinic was in the old part of Hendon. Dad had often taken me there on various errands and I knew it well. I recall many disabled men sitting on the pavements, often with no legs, sometimes blind or badly scarred from burns or old wounds. Crutches were lying at their sides. They were begging for money or morsels of food – sad reminders of the Great War which had ended only two decades earlier and which was still strongly embedded in adult memory.

Another street memory from those days was the organ grinder who produced mechanical music by turning a large handle at the side of the organ. A battered old cloth cap lay nearby, slowly filling with coppers thrown in by passers-by who had been lured by a tiny monkey wearing a bright red fez on his head and sitting atop the organ. Prompted by my father I asked the monkey's name. 'Jacky' was the reply. Ever since then I have nurtured an abhorrence of being called Jacky as I always think of it as a monkey's name!

On the way home from the clinic Mum explained that we had been injected with a substance to keep us fit and well during our journey.

'What journey?'

'The long journey on a big boat.'

'When?'

'Quite soon.'

'Why?'

'You are going to stay with Uncle Maurice while the war lasts. You are very lucky – you will be happy and safe with him.'

'Where does he live?'

'New Zealand.'

I was perplexed. I had never heard of Uncle Maurice, nor of a place called New Zealand.

'Where is New Zealand?'

'It is a long way away, across the water.'

Perhaps it was her use of the word 'water' rather than 'sea' which threw me, but I spent quite a while after that puzzling over which lake or river Mum was referring to.

My little brother soon worked out it was the Thames. After we had crossed the river at the top of a double-decker bus, he asked in his high loud voice, 'Are we in New Zealand now?' I wondered why everyone in the bus smiled.

Soon afterwards Nanna, who kept us supplied in woollen garments throughout our childhood, knitted little jumper suits in mottled grey and brown for Bronia and me. As we tried them on it was explained that they were for the sea journey.

But suddenly all talk of the trip ceased. Days before we were due to sail, a ship carrying evacuees was torpedoed by German U-boats, despite having a huge red cross painted on its side to identify it as a civilian vessel, rather than a warship. S.S. *Benares* sailed from Liverpool for Canada on 13th September 1940 with more than one hundred child evacuees aboard. It sank on 17th September. Of the people on board 256 drowned, including about eighty children, while thirty-one children survived, having been tossed into lifeboats, and returned home feted as heroes. The overseas evacuation scheme was immediately stopped. I nursed vague feelings of being let down and of missing out on an exciting adventure.

It was only after having children of my own that I realised the enormity of the sacrifice my parents had been prepared to make. Sending one's children abroad must have been a dreadfully agonising decision. They could not have known when, if ever, they were likely to see us again, but apparently they had thoughts about joining us in New Zealand after the war. Most children who were evacuated abroad had no conception of the reality of the situation and were totally unaware that a possible six years of separation from loved ones lay ahead.

Over forty years later I asked her how she would have coped with her emotions and the trauma of seeing her young family sail away. She looked at me in silence for a few moments, unable to speak. Instead, her eyes moistened and a solitary tear trickled slowly down her cheek. Realising I had stirred deep painful feelings long repressed, I changed the subject. I never referred to it again.

We were to learn more about Uncle Maurice and his family in the years to come. He was not actually an uncle, but Dad's first cousin whose family had emigrated to New Zealand in 1913 when he was but a lad of six. In 1940 he had a small daughter who used to watch the passenger liners sailing into Wellington Harbour, wondering which one we were on. After his initial letter to my parents offering to have us for the duration of the war, he and his wife regularly sent us food parcels and little gifts, especially at Christmas.

My interest in this far-flung branch of the family having been awakened, I began writing to them regularly, vowing that one day I would make that journey to New Zealand. It was not until 1975 that I was able to do so for the first time, and to meet the family which so very nearly became my own.

* * *

30

Jacqueline, Michael and Bronia in our neglected back garden in 1941.
The entrance to the Anderson shelter can just be seen back left.

Radio began to do a magnificent job in helping to raise our spirits. Programmes like *Music While You Work* were broadcast to keep up morale in factories. *Workers' Playtime* was composed of groups of entertainers who toured factories and workshops, broadcasting from the canteens. There were excellent comedy shows to get the nation laughing. I was nine by now, reading newspapers and listening to the radio like everyone else, becoming more aware of what was going on.

We were all preparing and bracing ourselves for the expected invasion, wondering when it would start. But we felt all was ready – we had dear old Winnie at the helm now, more than a match for that little twerp across the sea. What a blessing we did not realise just how *unready* we in fact were. The general mood would have been very different had we known the truth.

3

This Is It

Without warning, war arrived on the Home Front in the late summer of 1940. The exact date eludes me but we happened to be visiting Grandpa Hollings in New Malden at the time. Grandpa had driven our family from there to Teddington for the afternoon to enjoy a lazy boat trip on the Thames in warm sunshine. This peaceful idyll was unexpectedly shattered by the blood-curdling sound of a wailing siren which we knew was the air-raid Alert. We had to find cover immediately but were caught in the middle of the river. Frantic rowing got us quickly to the bank where we joined other groups of people in a boat-house, the only shelter we could find. Worry and concern were expressed on their pale faces; frightened children were clinging to parents. No one knew what best to do or what to expect. Parents' instincts were to get children home as soon as possible, but common sense dictated that we stay put until we heard the All Clear siren.

The thuds, bumps and bangs of an air raid could be heard in the distance; sounds that would become all too familiar in the weeks to come. We felt curiously safe clustered together inside the boat-house but everyone was thoughtful and quiet.

Eventually, after two or so long hours, the All Clear sounded and we made our way back to the car with relief but totally unprepared for the sights that met us as we drove slowly along New Malden High Street. Many shops had been flattened, and there were scenes of chaos amid dust and piles of rubble.

Grandpa's house around the corner was intact, but we were all still in a state of shock as we returned home later to Colindale by bus and tube, reflecting what might have been had we stayed in New Malden instead of deciding to spend the afternoon in a boat.

That was our last journey to South London for a very long time.

* * *

Our Anderson shelter in the garden now proved its worth as we began to sleep in it regularly. It had been made as cosy as possible by Dad, with Mum adding her own homely little touches. The air-raids were increasing in number and often disturbed our sleep. A wailing siren warned us of German planes approaching over Kent, and was soon followed by a cacophony of various noises, low drones of plane engines, boomphs, bangs, bumps and thuds of bombs near and far, windows rattling from a blast, shaking walls, quivering earth tremors, whines of descending bombs, and the constant crack-crack of the anti-aircraft guns (which we found strangely comforting). All this was accompanied by flashes in the sky, and the beams of searchlights scanning across it looking for planes. A tremendous feeling of relief always followed the All Clear, a one-note siren, but often that was short-lived when another raid came soon after.

Gradually people learned to cope and became more prepared for the nightly interruptions. The surface brick shelter at the entrance to our cul-de-sac was now in full use night after night. Two women fought over what they considered to be the safest bed in a corner, each competing with the other to grab it first. In the end they fell out completely, not speaking to each other for years. This was the exception for most people were very friendly, helping each other as troubles, worries and difficulties arose.

There was a wonderful spirit of camaraderie. People saw the funny side of things, remaining surprisingly happy and resilient despite the most harrowing situations, hardships and suffering. No one ever doubted that we would finally win the war, even during the darkest days.

We all worked together to achieve that end, even children. Michael joined Bronia and me in learning to knit. We bought lots of khaki coloured wool to knit scarves for soldiers, navy wool for sailors, and sometimes knitted various coloured squares which were sewn together for blankets.

* * *

By now, Dad was a Royal Marine stationed at Dover, and undertook spells of duty manning the anti-aircraft guns on top of the cliffs. He was to shoot down as many enemy aircraft as possible as they flew over the coast, before they could drop their bombs on London. We lay awake in the shelter, wakened by the sirens and other raid-related noises, listening intently and fearfully to the various tones of plane engines. We became skilled in detecting the difference between Theirs and Ours. When one of Theirs droned overhead we shouted, 'You missed *that* one Daddy!'

In London's East End, an Anderson Shelter remains intact amidst destruction and debris after a landmine fell nearby. The three people who had been inside the shelter were unhurt.
(© Imperial War Museum D5949)

We were rarely aware of Mum sleeping in the shelter, because of the curtain perhaps, or because we were asleep by the time she joined us. But looking back I do wonder whether she really did sleep there very often. Her asthma made her hate small enclosed spaces so perhaps she avoided the shelter whenever possible.

One incident stands out. We were all asleep in the shelter about 2 a.m. when I was awakened by Mum groping around for the torch, slowly creaking open the door and crawling into the garden. Some while later, still awake and mystified, I felt something run through my hair and over my pillow. A mouse! So that was it.

I admired Mum's self-control in remaining so quiet for

she detested the creatures. Although I did not share her fear of mice, I had no desire to share my bed with one, so I also decided to leave the shelter and creep out. I had hardly settled into bed in the house when Bronia followed. Michael, I learned years later, was very indignant at finding himself alone when he awoke in the morning!

It was not until breakfast next morning that Mum realised we had followed her into the house. We had a good laugh about it although she never admitted to any knowledge of the little visitor.

It was years before we finally allowed her to forget the night she was far more scared of a little mouse than of Hitler's bombs!

* * *

Newspapers began to tell of fierce air battles over Kent. They weren't referring to it yet as the Battle of Britain, but we sensed its importance as we read of pilots' heroism, trying to force back the enemy and protect London and the nation from the Luftwaffe. Daily bulletins included lists of casualties and losses but there always seemed to be more losses on their side than ours. We suspected this was mere propaganda, but the reports were in fact accurate.

Often the dreaded sirens came during daytime, prompting a mad dash into the surface shelters. If we heard a falling bomb we fell flat on our faces to protect ourselves from the explosion, bracing ourselves for the boomph and shudder of its landing. One little boy continued to throw himself down at any sudden noise for some months after the war had ended; a habitual and entrenched reflex action which his mother found difficult to cure.

The raids steadily became more frequent, regularly occurring night after night. The sirens announcing that enemy planes had been spotted approaching the south coast woke us up at any time, but mostly between 9 p.m. and 2 a.m., often later. This meant a very sleepy and bleary-eyed populace having to make a supreme effort to get up next morning. It became the rule that if a raid continued after 3 a.m., school would start at 10 a.m. next day.

Each morning children found the streets littered with pieces of shrapnel (bomb splinters), which they collected. The largest, most spectacularly jagged bits were proudly displayed on the mantelpiece as ornaments. Boys especially would compete with each other for the best pieces, but this was discouraged because sometimes small unexploded shells or bombs were left lying around proving very tempting for children. For example, we were warned via school talks and posters not to touch the small oblong objects called Butterfly Bombs, as they could explode when handled or kicked – and often did.

Our school routine was disrupted by daytime raids. As soon as the Alert sounded, each class was led into the shelters at the far end of the field (for that is what the trench-mounds were which I had watched being built from my classroom). Each class had its own shelter. Along the side were uncomfortably hard wooden benches on which we had to sit and wait for the All Clear. After a few of these interruptions, letters were sent to parents suggesting that each child take a flat cushion to school, with a tuck box of basic rations, possibly a card game and also a long pencil rubber. The latter was to insert between the teeth of the child should he suffer from fear or hysteria.

For each of us Mum made a cushion folded from a square piece of old blanket, using one of the folds to form a pocket to hold the rubber, a game of Snap, an apple and a biscuit. She added a handle to make carrying easier. Her design was unique and served its purpose well.

We were not far into the autumn term before the school suddenly closed due to the discovery of an unexploded shell embedded into the corner of a classroom. It was closed for eight weeks. During that time small classes were held in some of the children's homes, parents having volunteered use of their living rooms for a week at a time on a rota basis. I remember reciting the eight times table, being one of a class of twelve children sitting around my own living room.

Every parent who had participated in this emergency arrangement received a potted plant from the teacher as a thank you. Each house was used twice. A little boy at number six had pulled all the large red berries off his mother's pot-plant after his class's first week at his house. When the second week came round, little did his teacher realise that all the berries were fixed onto the plant with sewing pins!

The nation took its new King and Queen to their hearts after they toured bomb damage in the East End of London, and talked at length to the people. King George VI and Queen Elizabeth were much admired for not leaving London during the Blitz, despite Buckingham Palace being bombed and badly damaged.

* * *

Throughout the Blitz I continued the Saturday morning journeys by tube train to the Guildhall School of Music in Blackfriars for piano lessons. I became very used to the journey which was surprisingly rarely interrupted by an air-raid, thank goodness, but I could see the aftermath of the previous week's nightly destruction as I emerged into the street from the Underground. After the lesson I sometimes wandered the streets near St Paul's Cathedral and found gaps where buildings had stood, craters, dust, rubble, smoke and piles of debris.

In those days there were no automatic doors on the Metropolitan Line trains. Being so small I found it very difficult to find the strength to pull down the big heavy handles that opened the doors, and found myself having to go on to the next station a few times. I then walked back to Blackfriars along Queen Victoria Street, seeing yet more devastation.

Fire fighters tackling a blaze after an air-raid in Queen Victoria Street, Blackfriars, Central London. (© Imperial War Museum HU1129)

My most vivid memories of the Saturday trips remain those of the central London tube stations being utilised as shelters. The platforms were covered with sleeping men, women, and children cuddling their teddies, some on crude bunk beds, and of family groups eating sandwiches, brewing tea and heating soup on camp stoves. I had to pick my way through them and over their belongings to reach the exit. The impression was of a huge jumble of humanity covering each platform.

During one awfully tragic night, many people were killed while making their way down into Bethnal Green Underground tube station for shelter. One person slipped at the top of the stairs causing a domino reaction, which crushed everyone below, resulting in 178 fatalities. 177,000 people regularly used the Underground shelters at night. During the Blitz nearly 43,000 civilians were killed.

Civilians asleep in the Elephant and Castle tube station taking shelter from the raids above. November 1940.
(© Imperial War Museum HU672)

By now it was rare to see a young man out of uniform. Trains were crowded with soldiers carrying rifles and heavy oblong kit-bags, with their identification numbers stamped in big black numbers along the side.

The main roads were full of military trucks, vehicles and open lorries from which high-spirited young soldiers waved and whistled at pretty girls.

* * *

I first learned of 'Lord Haw-Haw' when I overheard a small group of women on a street corner laughing and jeering about a voice on the radio the previous evening saying, in menacing tones, 'You've got away with it so far, Hendon, but it is *your* turn next.' I found it puzzling that this ominous statement had caused merriment rather than fear, until Mum explained.

At first, very little information of the war's progress was given out in the media, so people began to tune in to German propaganda broadcasts from Hamburg searching for news. 'Doctor' Goebbels, the propaganda minister, cooperated with the German Foreign Office to plan programmes presenting the war in a favourable light for the German cause, and they tried to undermine British morale by half-truths, twisted truths and blatant untruths.

The British authorities were at first alarmed as to the possible effect these broadcasts would have, but after a while they were seen as harmless entertainment, and were treated with derisive scorn. The newsreaders, obviously English, weren't taken seriously and became a national joke, held in high contempt. ('Lord Haw-Haw' was at first used as a collective nickname for two or three of the readers, but later came to be applied to one man in particular, William Joyce, an Irish-British Fascist who had fled to

Germany at the outbreak of war. He became the most hated man of the war after Hitler, and was later captured, accused and convicted of Treason.)

* * *

One night we had a very close shave when a bomb landed in the next road. It landed in a clump of laurel bushes so did very little damage, although it made a heck of a thud when it hit the ground. We felt the vibrations within our shelter and were quite convinced we had lost our house. The sense of relief was overwhelming next morning when we saw it still standing.

Supervised by Mum, I was in the bath one evening when the air-raid Alert sounded slightly earlier than we had come to expect. We were about to empty the bath when we heard the dreaded shriek of a descending bomb, followed by the inevitable thud and bump, rattling of windows, and shaking of the very foundations of the house. I don't think anyone could have made it faster from bath to shelter than we did that night.

We heard next morning that a landmine had flattened Colindale Underground Station. There were two trains there at the time, both packed with airmen and nearly all were killed. We were becoming hardened and immune to news of casualties and sudden death, but that event stunned and upset us all, and brought home to us just what great danger we were in. I cannot now but help reflect that an incident like this would be treated as a major disaster in peacetime, but these tragedies were occurring almost every day with barely a two-line mention in the newspaper.

The legendary stoicism of the British was in evidence each morning. A neighbourly nod across a garden hedge would bring forth such pithy one-liners as 'A noisy night, eh?' or, 'Nearer this time!' Sometimes, 'Trying to knock the aerodrome out I suppose.' Defiantly, 'They're not getting me out of *my* home!' Then another nod was exchanged before continuing the day's business.

It was about this time that I asked Mum what would happen to us all if Hitler invaded our country. 'You two girls would be taken for Hitler's breeding programme', (we were too young to understand the implications). 'Michael would be forced to join the Hitler Youth Movement. All Jews, gypsies, the old, crippled, sick and insane would be done away with.' There was no need to continue. To everyone it was becoming increasingly obvious that Hitler was a raving lunatic who just had to be stopped.

One noisy night, knowing we were all awake, Mum called us into her bedroom to see a spectacular sight from her south-facing window. A vast part of central London was on fire. Beyond the stark silhouettes of nearby houses was a huge yellow glow, darkening gradually to bright orange through red to purple. It was barely believable as we all watched awe-struck. The whole sky was aglow. Mum remarked that we were witnessing history; we would remember this sight all our lives, and our grandchildren would read about it in books.

We cuddled together in our dressing-gowns watching for some time, wondering what incidents, tragedies and tales of heroism would be reported in the morning paper; and how much longer we would have to endure this traumatic and frightening state of affairs which had become everyday life for us.

* * *

The raids began to slacken off in early November 1940 and families were beginning to regain confidence that they could once more sleep uninterrupted in their own beds. News came of bombings and devastation in Birmingham and Coventry, later Plymouth, and London again in the new year, when Guildhall (not the music school) and St Bride's Church were damaged in a raid on the City.

Winston Churchill appealed to America for help in his 'Give us the tools and we'll finish the job' speech. The fear of invasion was still strong, but it was suspected that Hitler had missed his opportunity. Instead of invading us at the start of the war when we had been so unprepared, he marched into Norway. His armies then turned towards Eastern Europe, and by the summer of 1941 had entered Russia. The nation then breathed a sigh of relief, for an invasion of Britain now seemed unlikely for the present. We prayed that the English Channel, as in the past, would save us yet again.

4

We All Do Our Bit

We rarely saw Dad once he had joined the Royal Marines. I believe that he was first sent to Leigh-on-Sea for initial training, and Mum was allowed to join him there one weekend. He occasionally had a weekend at home while in England and, very rarely, a whole week's leave was granted which usually meant that his unit was due for overseas duty. He was stationed at Portsmouth and Chatham at various times but I was exceedingly vague about his wartime career.

Very little information was given to Mum, still less to us children. Secrecy was paramount. It was constantly drilled into us that we were never to discuss Dad's whereabouts with anyone. Posters on hoardings, in buses and trains warned, 'Ssh – Careless Talk Costs Lives'. It was assumed that Hitler's spies were everywhere.

We never knew in advance when Dad was coming home. The husband of the lady next door was also in the forces. Both she and Mum were awakened one night by the clump, clump, clump of heavy boots getting louder and louder. Each wife lay in her bed wondering whose boots they were. They belonged to Dad whom we hadn't seen for some months. Oh, the excitement that night! He was exhausted after carrying his kit-bag and rifle for many hours, much of it in the dark, but all that was forgotten in the joy of being at home with his family.

Our neighbour never heard her husband's boots again. He died of a fever in Madagascar.

* * *

Meanwhile the bombs and raids were having their effect on Nanna and her neighbours in Thornton Heath. Like others without a garden shelter, she felt that the cupboard under the stairs was the safest place during a raid. Once inside her stair cupboard, one neighbour was too frightened to come out even after the All Clear. She only emerged, white-faced and trembling, after much gentle coaxing and encouragement from Nanna, and gradually became a nervous wreck.

Most of the houses in that area suffered from bomb-damage, with some quite badly hit. After a while Nanna and Grandpa could stand no more and decided to move. It seems odd in retrospect, but they moved to Lancing on the south coast near Worthing, renting a two-bedroomed bungalow until their house could be sold. With her usual zest for life she had soon thrown herself into many local activities. Before long she was President of the Women's Institute, learning how to can fruit and make leather goods. In the local drama club she found an outlet for her suppressed acting talent, surprising the family with her emergence as a comedienne. Her portrayal of Grandma Buggins became a local hit. She was a natural, but never understood why she was inevitably cast in that role. She revelled in all the admiration and was at her humorous best when the centre of attention.

Being in possession of exceptionally green fingers, her little garden was soon ablaze with colour, and full of fruit bushes. Gladioli were her speciality and every year she entered a few for flower competitions. Grandpa, much older than his wife, was a very quiet man who spent most of his time sunk into a big armchair reading the *Daily Mail* and smoking his pipe. He had an allotment nearby but it gradually became too much for him and he eventually abandoned it.

In the summer of 1941 when the fear of invasion was still strong, Nanna kept a pitchfork in her shed. One day, adopting an aggressive and threatening stance with it she announced, 'I'm ready for 'em! They won't get past me!' This was typical of the mood of anger and indignation that people felt against anyone who contemplated an invasion of these shores. Any attempt to do so would have been met with total defiance and very bitter resistance.

Nanna's bungalow in Lancing showing Mum,
Michael, Jacqueline and Bronia. 1942.

* * *

49

By now the south and east coasts were forbidden zones, the beaches totally out of bounds, protected by rolls and rolls of barbed-wire to keep people away from the dangers of hidden mines and other protective measures against possible invasion. Along the seashore were placed huge concrete cube blocks to deter enemy tanks from swarming over the beaches.

Before we could visit Nanna we had to apply for a special permit, which was granted because she was a close relative. Conditions of war allowing, each August we children spent three or four weeks in Lancing. Because the pleasures of the sea were denied to us, we turned inland and discovered the delights of the Downs instead. We took picnic lunches to our favourite spot overlooking Lancing and the village of Sompting, a hilly slope with a backdrop of trees and bushes. From there we enjoyed the spectacular view of Brighton and the white cliffs of Beachy Head to our left, across the wide vista of sea to Worthing and Selsey Bill to our right. The trees provided scope for games such as hide-and-seek. We also enjoyed bus rides to Clapham Woods, Arundel Castle, Brighton and Eastbourne; a whole new wonderful world opened up to us away from the confines of poor, sad, bomb-shattered London.

Attached to the rear of the bungalow was a glass conservatory with shelves covered with pot-plants at one end and a healthy thriving vine at the other. We often ate tea of cucumber sandwiches there, accompanied by noisy bluebottles flying around in the hot sun under the glass. Nearly seventy years later the buzz, buzz of a blue-bottle still prompts the taste and smell of cucumber.

The large black grapes were delicious. Conveniently for us our bedroom window opened out into that end of the conservatory. I could lie on the upper bunk bed and reach out through the open window to pick as many grapes as conscience allowed. Only one bunch went the first night. As it was not missed, the following night we picked a bunch each. By the end of the week the vine was totally stripped of its grapes. We lay low, waiting for the anger and punishment that surely must follow, but Nanna said nothing. Instead, she guaranteed future protection of the grapes by rearranging the bedrooms!

The same fate soon befell her prize gooseberry bushes. One morning, after preparing pastry for a pie, she went into the garden to pick a bowlful of gooseberries and found the bushes naked. Not only had the lovely soft red ones gone, but the green also. This time her frustration caused a rare burst of anger, followed by silent treatment for two days. That was enough to ensure that we never again robbed her of fruit; but they were the most scrumptious gooseberries I have ever tasted!

* * *

After much of the garden in Colindale had been turned over to chickens, it became a constant battle keeping rodents away. One or two were shot, but that did little to control them so it was decided to keep a cat. A tabby joined us, but became ill and died after only eighteen months. Next came Chloe, a beautiful black and white specimen.

To my father cats were a menace, to be tolerated only because of their value in discouraging rats and mice. His main grumble was that they scratched and dug up seedlings and disturbed young plants. We often heard him mutter 'that damn cat!', so it was no surprise that he was very annoyed to learn, during one leave home, that Chloe was pregnant. The thought of even more of the 'damn things' appalled him.

The night before her kittens were due, Chloe had organised herself into a comfortable warm hollow on Bronia's bed, but Mum gently lifted her downstairs into a box filled with straw. Chloe's indignant protests were echoed by both Bronia's and mine, to no avail.

Very early next morning we crept downstairs and were surprised to find Dad leaning over the box, still in his pyjamas, gently stroking Chloe and talking lovingly and soothingly to her. Her very loud purrs could be heard upstairs as she licked each tiny kitten. Dad was not known for displays of tenderness and so, embarrassed at being caught, he dashed upstairs trying to hide his loss of composure by muttering, 'Yes, well... er... I just came down to make a cup of tea.'

Chloe's four kittens grew into the prettiest quartet ever of fluff, fun and frolic. How we all loved and enjoyed those kittens! We brought our school friends home to see them and, when they were old enough, we took the kittens into the garden to play. Neighbours watched from their windows, also enjoying the kittens' mad helter-skelter. Cleo, Blackie, Figaro and Mitzi created a happy diversion from matters of war, and the delight they gave us increased as they grew.

One day I arrived home from school to find a strange stillness in the house. Soon realising the kittens were missing I began a frantic but fruitless search. Mum sorrowfully explained that, as they were getting bigger, she could no longer afford to feed them so she had offered them to the Navy, who planned to take them on board a warship to keep rats at bay.

Silence greeted this unexpected revelation until one of us asked where was Chloe? 'She had to go too so the kittens wouldn't miss her.' It was not long before the obvious truth dawned but I said nothing, preferring to believe that our kittens too, in their own small way, were helping the war effort.

We all missed them.

* * *

The nation was at a very low ebb during 1941. Hitler had conquered most of Europe and was now advancing into Russia. Britain and Russia entered into a pact to help each other, and Mrs Churchill started her Aid to Russia fund. Now that Hitler's attention was elsewhere the threat of invasion receded and we all breathed more freely for a while.

Clothes rationing arrived; so did a plague of caterpillars brought on, no doubt, by the thousands of allotments everywhere, with all those inviting cabbages. After the Cabbage White had gorged its way through the depleted vegetation and was fat enough to search for a suitable place to pupate, the great migration began. At Lancing I was confronted by hoards and hoards of caterpillars wriggling across from fields on one side of the road to fences on the other. It was impossible to proceed without treading on them, so I had to pick my way very carefully on tiptoe.

Mum did her best to keep our allotment going when Dad was absent but found it difficult with three youngsters, her Food Office job and bouts of asthma attacks. We spent a lot of time helping her remove caterpillars from the plants, the quickest method being to grab handfuls to drop into a bucket of salt solution. (I preferred to knock them off the leaves one by one at the end of a very long stick, but was ticked-off for not pulling my weight.)

* * *

Apart from cinema and radio there was not much entertainment during the war, which is why the Saturday night dances were so popular. These were held in village or church halls to the records of Henry Hall, Geraldo, Glen Miller, Joe Loss, Jack Payne and their bands. Most of the men were in uniform on leave, relaxing from the tensions of war. I was far too young to attend the dances and envied the older girls who seemed to have such fun.

Cinemas were popular. It was estimated that the total weekly audience was made up of 25–30 million people. Each programme consisted of the main film, a lesser feature or 'B-film', a newsreel depicting the latest events in the war, short documentaries and information films. Once inside the cinema we could sit through the main film again if we wished, as the programmes were continuous.

The Government soon realised the value of cinema to get its messages across, so the Ministry of Information produced short features for imparting advice on such issues as raids, allotments, spies, unexploded bombs and healthy eating.

Morale-boosting films appeared which were honest representations of the war, e.g. *In Which We Serve*, the true story of H.M.S. *Kelly*. They were semi-documentary as well as being entertaining. Comedies were thought to be essential for keeping spirits high and were churned out regularly.

There were also Saturday morning cinema clubs for children, containing cartoons, short films and serials based on popular characters from comics. I attended these for a while but found the audiences too noisy, deafening the soundtrack, and I soon lost interest.

A party was once given in our local church hall for children of absent servicemen. Bronia, Michael and I were

WE ALL DO OUR BIT

invited. I cannot recall if it was Christmas-time but we had paper hats, balloons, a tea party, games, a conjurer and competitions.

* * *

We continued knitting scarves for servicemen, and woollen squares for Mum to sew into blankets. More experienced knitters made balaclava helmets, socks and gloves, mostly in khaki for the Army. These were collected by the WVS for distribution where needed, the blankets going to the homeless, air-raid victims, children's homes, casualty needs, Red Cross, and so on.

Our recently widowed neighbour knitted us a doll each, dressed beautifully as soldier, sailor or airman. Michael was given the sailor, me the airman: which proved prophetic in its way, as Michael later joined the Navy for his two years' conscription, and I married an ex-airman.

* * *

Mum and her friend at No. 6 conceived the rather ambitious idea of producing and presenting a concert in the style of one of those pre-war concert parties held at the end of a seafront pier. Proceeds were to go to Mrs Churchill's Aid to Russia fund. The entertainment was provided entirely by the children of our road, and Mum organised sketches, choreographed dance sequences, found suitable songs and choruses and designed the costumes.

All the mothers fully cooperated, pooling their clothing coupons to buy enough bright blue and yellow material to make their own child's Pierrot costume. Each child was dressed in tunic or trousers, topped with a conical hat decorated by large pompoms.

Rehearsals were held in each others' houses with the

usual traumas, tantrums, worries and panics, but it all come together eventually. The venture was a success. We gave two performances in a local hall, each attended by a large, appreciative and generous audience. Every one of the eight children had a solo item; singing, tap-dancing, recitation or piano solos, in addition to group items and routines involving the whole company.

It is amazing what children can achieve with enthusiastic coaching, goodwill, coordinated effort and cooperation.

The cast of the Concert Party given by some of the children of our road to support Mrs Churchill's Aid to Russia fund. Jacqueline is fourth from the left behind Bronia. Michael is second from the right.

* * *

Before Christmas in 1941 the Japanese had bombed the American Naval Base at Pearl Harbor and declared war on USA and Britain, prompting President Roosevelt to declare war on Germany and Italy. So at last we had a strong ally on our side and felt more hopeful of a successful outcome eventually, although we had a long way yet to go.

The German armies had reached Moscow, H.M.S. *Ark*

Royal had been sunk, the Japanese had overrun Hong Kong, so things were still looking very bleak. In January 1942 they invaded Burma, and by the summer the Germans were in North Africa.

* * *

My parents developed a code that Dad used in his letters home to give clues to Mum as to when he was going overseas. His letters usually began 'Dearest', but if he was to be posted abroad he wrote 'Dear Dorothy'.

A letter arrived 'Dear Dorothy' in the spring of 1942. It was a long time before we heard any further news, even longer before we learned where he was, and an eternity before we saw him again.

5

Will It Never End?

As the war dragged on, radio played an increasingly prominent part in the nation's life. Daily news bulletins were a must, and the special record request programmes for the Forces were very popular, containing messages from servicemen overseas for their folks at home. We all hung on to Churchill's every word whenever one of his speeches was broadcast.

Comedians of the day kept us all laughing, raising morale. There were many, but the favourite by far was Tommy Handley whose programme *ITMA* ('*It's That Man Again*') was so popular it was on three times each week. Meals were served to coincide with his broadcasts so families could eat, chuckle and laugh together. Who can ever forget the much-loved characters of Mrs Mopp ('Can I do you now, Sir?'), Mona Lott, Colonel Chinstrap, Claud and Cecil, Funf (the German spy), Mr Handlebar, Ally Oop and the diver who, descending among gurgly bubbles, always implored, 'Don't forget the diver, Sir, don't forget the diver'?

ITMA was the first programme to introduce the new rapid-fire type of humour, and I therefore suppose it was the forerunner of the *Goon Show*. When Tommy Handley's sudden death was announced not long after the war, the whole nation deeply felt the loss. The BBC was often asked to repeat *ITMA* during the following years but it was explained that the gags and jokes were so topical that a new audience would not have found them funny. They were probably right, but those of us who heard them the first time would have loved a second chance to enjoy them.

Other favourites were Arthur Askey in *Bandwaggon*, Jack (blue pencil) Warner, and dear old Rob Wilton whose monologues in his unhurried lazy drawl always began, 'The day war broke out, my missus said to me, she said, "What are you going to *do* about it?" "About what?" "The *war*, you've got to *do* something",' by which time I was helpless.

The radio regularly broadcast names from the latest casualty lists. It was via one of these programmes that we learned of the death of a grandson of Nanna's cousin. It was a great shock suddenly hearing his name on the list of those killed in action.

Children's Hour was a great favourite for us. We enjoyed listening to 'Uncle Mac' who always ended his programmes with, 'Goodnight children – everywhere'. We found his voice very comforting.

Radio programmes were often linked by a tuning signal based on the three treble notes B-B-C. Also used was the motif from the first movement of Beethoven's fifth symphony. It happened to be the same rhythm as the Morse code signal for the letter V, 'dot dot dot dash' (...-). Beethoven stood for the rights of man, individual freedom and a fair deal for the oppressed, ideas all reflected in much of his music. He would have been very proud to learn that his valiant little rhythmic motif was being used as the 'V for Victory' call throughout Europe.

* * *

Along the south coast many of the now empty houses were requisitioned for use by the Army. The soldiers needed canteens, and these were organised and staffed by the WVS. Nanna helped with catering and serving in the canteen on Lancing front. Volunteers worked on a rota-basis, which meant Nanna being involved two afternoons a week, but she baked pies, tarts and cakes at home to take to the canteen.

We often went along with her to help, so got to know several of the soldiers billeted there. I remember one in particular, a sandy-haired reserved youngster named Tommy Swain. Nanna befriended him because he seemed lonely, not given to mixing with the others.

One Christmas (maybe 1942) when our family were together in Lancing, Nanna invited several soldiers and a couple of lasses from the village to share our Christmas dinner and the celebrations afterwards. It was during that afternoon I was introduced to the fun of Postman's Knock, Murder in the Dark, John Brown's Body and other games. I was too young to appreciate their potential for frivolous flirtation and harmless frolics, but the young adults took full advantage of the opportunities, entering into the spirit of the occasion and having a marvellous time.

The soldiers stayed until well past midnight. Tommy had no folks of his own and adopted us as his family, keeping in touch with us for several months. Sadly, we later learned that he was killed during bitter fighting on the Continent. We were thankful that he had enjoyed a fun family Christmas at least once in his short unhappy life.

* * *

It must have been about this time that Nanna decided to acquire a few ducklings. While they were tiny it was easy to provide them with enough water for swimming. She dug a shallow hole to support a large upturned dustbin lid which contained sufficient water for a little pond. When Nanna wasn't looking we loved to cuddle and nurse the ducklings. I have no idea what later became of them. One supposes that they provided many eggs and a few dinners, but they couldn't have remained happy for long without a larger area of water.

* * *

Understandably, the war condition was reflected in the toys of the day. Michael spent hours on the floor directing his mini searchlights onto the ceiling, searching for imaginary planes, and firing tiny shells from realistic anti-aircraft guns at model aeroplanes suspended from the ceiling by string. The guns were adjustable to all angles and swivelled around on a base.

Little grey metal bombs had explosive 'caps' inserted into them before being dropped onto the pavement where they 'exploded' with a sharp crack, a sound which irritated grown-ups when repeated too often! The caps were bought in strips from toy shops and could also be fired in small toy pistols.

There were miniature toy tanks, military trucks, ambulances, lorries, etc. and metal personnel such as soldiers and nurses supported on a circular base and accompanied by props, e.g. stretchers.

Toy parachutes were popular, opening out effectively when dropped from an upstairs window. Michael once tried to make a parachute for himself using an old umbrella, and was preparing to jump out of an upstairs window to test it when Mum prevented him just in time. Wartime characters, themes and motifs began to appear on playing cards. Dolls were dressed in uniforms. Also popular was a board game picturing the faces of leading Nazis around its border, surrounding that of Hitler in the centre. It was hung on a wall, then darts were aimed at it. Scores were gained according to which Nazi was hit. A successful shot at Hitler gained the maximum mark. Goering (Head of the Luftwaffe) and Ribbentrop (Foreign Minister) also had high scores. Goebbels (Propaganda Minister) and Himmler (S.S. leader) scored lower. I think Eichmann was the lowest.

There was another version of this game with rubber rings thrown onto hooks - less dangerous than dart throwing. Such games would be frowned upon now, but at the time they seemed a harmless outlet for our hatred of Hitler, his Nazis and all the evil they represented. Pictures and films of Hitler addressing vast crowds at rallies or reviewing his troops prompted much derision, scorn and laughter. Children took delight in mocking him by marching around with their right arms raised, shouting 'Heil Hitler!', and goosestepping like his army, which we all thought looked ridiculous. All this was good for morale.

* * *

During the war all forces' mail was strictly censored to prevent the enemy obtaining clues giving them vital information on troop movements, battle plans, the whereabouts and size of army units and battalions. Although Dad was always careful what he wrote home, so many words had been cut out of some of his letters that they arrived looking like pieces of delicate lace.

Dad on leave at home with Mum.

Even so, previously arranged codes between Mum and Dad informed us that during the autumn and winter of 1942–43 he was in North Africa, which meant he was now deeply involved in one of the most bitterly fought campaigns of the war. There were long gaps between the arrival of his letters when we had no idea if he was alive or not, but we knew from newspapers and radio that General Montgomery's Eighth Army (the 'Desert Rats') was battling

64

it out with the Germans at El Alamein, eventually winning our first great victory.

After this victory Montgomery was held in very high esteem and affectionately known as 'Monty'.

With the landings of the British and Americans in North Africa and the defeat of Rommel, the war turned at last in our favour. This was a significant victory and there was much rejoicing at home. In January 1943 the Eighth Army captured Tripoli, and in May the Allies finally pushed the Germans out of North Africa.

Meanwhile the Germans had surrendered to Russians at Stalingrad, and there was talk at home of the war surely being over by Christmas. People were impatiently wondering why there was a delay in liberating Europe, and the slogan 'Start the Second Front Now' began to appear everywhere on walls, scrawled in white paint.

* * *

Mum procured a large map of Europe and North Africa to fix on to the living room wall, and bought little flags from Woolworths depicting the Union Jack, Stars and Stripes, Hammer and Sickle, Swastika and the flags of Italy and France. They were mounted on pins to stick into the map showing the latest positions of all the relevant armies.

Each morning we listened carefully to the radio news and studied newspaper reports before moving the flags accordingly. Depression set in if the Swastikas gained ground, elation if the Union Jack or Stars and Stripes advanced. Gradually all the Swastikas vanished from North Africa, and the Hammer and Sickles spread westward from Stalingrad. In July 1943 our little flags showed that the British and Americans had landed in Sicily and fully occupied the island one month later. (We learned afterwards that Dad was among the first to land in Sicily, and in Italy in September.)

* * *

At home many goods were becoming very scarce. There was a shortage of petrol, fuel, food and beer. Supplies of petrol were so low that experiments were made to run cars on gas. Huge ugly gas bags appeared on many car roofs. With the shortage of fuel came power cuts and neighbours again had to share ovens for cooking. Nothing was wasted. Clothes and material had been rationed by a points system in June 1941, except for working clothes. This caused enormous problems as children grew. We often wore cut down and adapted adult clothes. Garments were inherited from older girls in the neighbourhood, and in turn handed down to Bronia. We learned to make our own dresses from remnants of material, and alter dresses that had belonged to others.

The WVS helped distribute second-hand clothing among the needy. The Utility trademark on anything new guaranteed good basic design and high standards of workmanship at economic prices. Worn sheets were repaired by the 'sides-to-middle' method. Boy Scouts and Girl Guides helped with the collection and sorting of salvage – anything that could be rescued and used again. Life was very drab. Bright colours were rarely seen. Houses were painted in brown, black or dark green. Even the interiors were dull and cheerless. To this day I hate to see anything wasted. I still have only 6 inches of water in my bath; turn off all lights not in use; remain frugal with my use of gas and electricity; and never buy new if the old will still do. I also still shudder with fear whenever I hear a wailing siren – feelings and habits still deeply entrenched within me and, I suspect, with most people of my generation who lived through the war years.

One of the jobs of council workers was to search for empty houses, or occupied houses with a spare room, which could be requisitioned for the use of US Servicemen. They knocked on our door more than once asking if we could house an airman but Mum had to turn them down.

Michael had a school friend living near Hendon Aerodrome whose family took in two airmen. One of them started courting the beautiful sixteen-year-old at No. 8, other residents in the road following the flowering romance with interest and not just a little envy. Widespread consternation followed their engagement ('far too young'), but as soon as the war ended June became one of the thousands of young war brides of American servicemen who settled in the United States, her mother and younger sister later joining her. I often wondered how she fared in her new life.

People were beginning to notice how fit and bonny all the babies were looking. At the start of the war the Ministry of Food had begun to issue concentrated orange juice and cod liver oil, via the welfare clinics, to all children under five to supplement the meagre food rations. It soon made a dramatic difference to children's basic health.

There were long queues at shops for essential foods, but it became an unwritten rule that all the pregnant and elderly be served first, and usually were.

* * *

We had a very reliable electric chiming clock in our living room, which had given trouble-free service since the day it was bought soon after Mum and Dad married in 1930. One day it suddenly stopped for no apparent reason.

Immediately looking concerned and pale, Mum said, 'Oh no – Daddy's in trouble'.

Not long after, she received official notification that Dad had become seriously ill with malaria, on the very day the clock had stopped, and had been taken from the front line in Italy back to hospital in North Africa. It seemed odd that Mum should link the clock with Dad's welfare, but it was from incidents such as these that we became aware of her uncannily accurate premonitions and highly perceptive sixth sense which rarely let her down.

As soon as he was well enough to travel Dad arrived home on extended sick leave, armed with several bottles of quinine to treat the expected recurring attacks of malaria. He told us of his ordeal and of being so ill; how he was lying in bed one night soaking in deep pools of per-spiration, in a partial coma, when he overheard one nurse whisper to another, 'No need to sponge him down – he'll be dead by morning.'

He remembered thinking 'Oh, will I?', and mustered all his mental energy, determination and stubborn will to survive the night and prove the nurse wrong. It was not his first close shave with death and was not to be his last. His recovery amazed the doctors and, despite all warnings, the malaria never returned. Our clock started again as mys-teriously as it had stopped, and was still going strong forty-six years later.

Dad had started the war with thick black wavy hair. He returned from the desert with it nearly all gone. What remained was greyish, thinning and straight, reflecting all the stress and trauma he had been through. He seemed to lead a charmed life while abroad, and had a few tales to tell of near misses, swopped duties and sheer luck saving his life.

In his kit-bag was a badly dented buckle from his belt. It

had saved him when a German charged straight at him with a bayonet. In another incident we would have lost Dad if he had not swopped guard duty with a marine, who was then blown up by a shell while on guard.

We were very proud to learn that Dad had been promoted to Lance Corporal, and were in awe of the stripe sewn onto his jacket. But he later returned it after he had refused to obey an order to place another marine on duty. As the man was very ill at the time Dad refused to do so and he demoted himself. However, he left the service after the war with a report which described his character as 'exemplary' so his transgression was forgiven.

After a few welcome weeks at home regaining his strength, Dad was pronounced fit enough to resume active service. At the end of his leave we all accompanied him to King's Cross station to say our goodbyes. It was the first time we had done this. I was not aware of his immediate destination, but the station platforms were crowded with servicemen kissing wives, children and sweethearts, and the train windows were alive with waving arms and fluttering handkerchiefs.

Once we had returned home Mum said it was suspected that Dad was being sent back to the battlefields, hence the extra lingering and tearful farewell at the station.

6

Here We Go Again

Calls to start the Second Front (allied invasion of the Continent) were becoming increasingly vociferous, but an operation of that magnitude had to be planned with maximum secrecy and meticulous attention to detail, and could not be entered into until all was absolutely ready.

We had noticed that troop movements and activity were increasing at Lancing and all along the coast. Military convoys and vehicles were clogging up the roads, taking precedence over, and often delaying, civilian traffic. Rumours abounded as we entered 1944. We all knew that the allied invasion to liberate Europe could not be far off, and waited for it with impatience because it would mean the beginning of the end for Hitler and his maniacal policies.

* * *

September 1942 had seen the start of my senior education at a girls' grammar school in Hampstead Garden Suburb. The journey to school took an hour, including a forty-minute ride on a trolley-bus which was motivated by wires strung overhead, linked to the bus's roof by a long pole. I had a mountain of homework each evening, which meant

Off to senior school. My first day as a pupil at Henrietta Barnett Girls'
Grammar School in Hampstead Garden Suburb,
north west London, 1942.

bedtime getting later and later, but I soon adjusted to these
changes. Bronia joined me one year later.

I was not happy at school. Although I did well acade-
mically, I was a failure socially, being too serious and quiet
to mix well with the more exuberant self-confident girls,
who took a cruel delight in seeing me put down, laughed
at or snubbed. They soon tagged me 'Pixie' because of my
petite stature. If they expected that to annoy me they were
disappointed. I quite liked the name. I was surprised to
find I was the only girl in my class with a father young
enough to be in military service.

I was too shy to make close friends but I enjoyed singing

in the choir (which broadcast once on *Children's Hour*), occasionally performing a piano solo at concerts, and accompanying a talented flautist, which meant visiting her home near the school for rehearsals.

School dinners reflected the austere diet of the day. There was lots of tasteless sponge pudding containing hard stringy dates, and apple pie sprinkled over-generously with cloves. A girl named Eva loved them. After the meal she collected everyone else's cloves and ate them all at once, making us shudder, wince, and turn our puckered faces away in disgust. Tapioca pudding was unpopular and rice was never cooked properly. I cannot remember much about the main course except for the peas. These were invariably hard as pellets, their colour but a pale apology for green. Each serving contained at least two boiled out maggot skins, but we survived, and looked surprisingly healthy on it!

* * *

The first few terms at senior school proceeded smoothly without incident. Then the air-raids started again and London groaned. We submitted patiently and with increased fortitude to a further onslaught from above, facing with fearful anticipation all the dreaded consequences.

The raids were sparse at first but gradually increased in frequency and severity. A big difference between these raids and those of 1940 was that all the rescue services were now better organised.

Unexploded bombs became a serious problem. After each was discovered people had to be evacuated from their homes and all surrounding roads roped off. Those marvellously brave and heroic bomb disposal experts then arrived to defuse it. Sometimes a bomb lay undisturbed for weeks, months or even years. Three were uncovered near Dartford nearly fifty years after they were dropped.

It was back to the shelters for everybody. In addition to the Anderson shelters in gardens, there was an indoor type of shelter known as the Morrison. Looking like a large cage with the sides measuring approximately 7 x 5 x 3 ft, it was designed for sleeping in. During one rare visit to my great aunt's home in Chingford, six of us slept in a row inside one of them. (Actually sleep was impossible. We were kept awake by talking, laughing and interpreting all the air-raid noises.) They were considered strong enough to give adequate protection from flying debris, collapsing ceilings and falling masonry. They were not available until February 1941 – too late to have been of use during the 1940 Blitz.

There were no purpose-built shelters at school but there was a large hall and stage under which was a maze of dressing rooms. All girls and staff were herded down there to sit out each raid. The whole of our second year summer exams were held in the makeshift shelters, papers balanced precariously upon our laps. When we weren't taking exams we played paper and pencil games to test our general knowledge and supplement our classwork. By the end of June the raids were so frequent that we spent more time in the shelters than in the classrooms.

It was during our mole-like existence in this concrete labyrinth that my close friendship with Pat grew and flourished. Our surnames were adjacent in the class register so we invariably found ourselves sitting next to each other. We soon discovered that her birthday was the day before mine so it seemed that fate had thrown us together, forming a close bond which was to last fifteen years.

Pat was my saviour, my protector from the taunts and

74

mockery of others, my partner in laughter, my sharer of giggles at all and nothing, to the constant despair of our teachers. She was someone in whom I confided my most private thoughts and with whom I could ride out life's storms.

Her forte was tennis; mine was music. We each admired the other's skill, giving support whenever possible. I watched her during tournaments, even umpiring one of her matches; she attended my concerts. We gave each other moral support during visits to the school dentist. In my troubled teen years I don't know how I would have coped without her.

We both detested cookery lessons, which were held in the top floor of the school. Towards the end of the lesson two girls had to carry out a dustbin full of rubbish to empty into huge receptacles behind the school. For most it was a dreaded chore but not for Pat and me. We always volunteered for the job just to get out of the classroom! By the time we had got the dustbin down four flights of stairs, we were helpless with laughter.

We took as long as we could, sitting and chatting at each floor level. The green paint on walls and staircase must have been very badly scored before we were through. Once we deliberately let the dustbin lid roll down on its own to see how far it would go and how much noise it would make. The resulting clatter went beyond our wildest expectations, reverberating around the whole school. Heads popped out of classrooms looking for the cause of the din. We swore it had been an accident and never dared repeat the experiment.

My last four years at school were made more tolerable by our shared fun.

* * *

75

Rumours began to circulate that the Second Front had begun. The skies were filled with the constant drone of planes flying south, giving credence to the rumours. On 6th June 1944 the Allies at last landed on the beaches of Normandy, and so began the last phase of the war. With the Allies now in Rome and Normandy and the Russians advancing towards Germany in the East, the Allied grip was closing in around the Nazis on all fronts.

Hitler was panicking. He had new weapons up his sleeve and he decided to unleash them in a final attempt to demoralise Londoners and force a surrender. It did not work, but merely increased our anger and determination to see the mad tyrant obliterated.

It was nasty. A new noise arrived above us, which can only be described as a very deep humming drone. This new and frightening object resembled a flying bomb, was pilotless and programmed to end its flight somewhere near London or beyond. The aim seemed haphazard, causing widespread fear and concern.

With experience we learned that we were safe as long as its monotonous bass tones continued overhead, but once its engine became silent we knew it would drop. This sudden quiet was eerie. Panic followed as we ducked under furniture, dived into the nearest shelter, or fell flat on our faces and braced ourselves for whatever the expected crash would bring.

We soon attached nicknames to the horrendous things but 'doodlebug' was the one that stuck. Doodlebugs caused more devastation than bombs dropped from a plane. One, dropped on Edgeware in October, resulted in 5 fatalities and rendered 74 houses uninhabitable. These figures were typical. Over 10,000 of them were launched between June and September 1944, killing 6,184 people.

Emergency services were stretched to the limit. Service engineers worked round the clock to repair damage to gas/electricity/water supplies. Rescue squads, ambulance drivers, the Fire Brigade, police, WVS all sprang into action following each landed bug. By July doodlebugs were travelling further north, causing further evacuations of families from London.

The occasional heavily censored letter from Dad gave clues that he was in the thick of it in Northern France, but no details. (He had been in the second wave of landings in Normandy on 6th June.) Paris was liberated amid jubilation in August, Brussels in September. Dad was in Brussels for some time, billeted with a family who had two daughters the same ages as Bronia and I. Marie Elizabeth and Elizabeth Marie were encouraged to start a pen-friendship with us. A few letters were exchanged but contact did not last long because of the language difficulty. A letter arriving later, starting 'Dear Jacqueline, Bronia, Michael and Ann', gave us the clue that Dad had moved on to Antwerp.

* * *

Stories began to filter through of horrors uncovered by the liberating armies. In Europe's major cities soldiers found execution rooms and torture chambers, and starving sick Jews in concentration and death camps, with evidence of mass genocide. These stories were met at first with total disbelief. Surely, hopefully, they were mere propaganda? With the proof of photographs, newsreel films and eye-witness reports, incredulity gave way to stunned shock and disgust at such heinous atrocities.

There was intense revulsion that such abominable evil could exist in the twentieth century, that men could stoop so low and become so depraved as to commit such wicked deeds.

Royal Marine Commandos landing on a Normandy beach on 6th June 1944 – D Day. (© Imperial War Museum B5218)

There were also reports of a brave but failed attempt on Hitler's life. If successful it would have brought the war to a quicker end, preventing further loss of life.

* * *

Hitler's final desperate attempt to break our spirit and cause collapse of morale on the home front occurred in September. Rumours of rockets or rocket shells began to circulate, and became a reality in the autumn. The doodlebugs were labelled V1s, and the rockets V2s. They caused new sorts of bangs, huge deep craters, violent earth tremors and high numbers of casualties.

The arrival of the V2s was a new shock, and each one arrived without warning. They were 45 feet long, and 1,043 were launched killing 2,754 civilians, although not all reached their target. London lost 130,000 homes – the damage was extensive. A total of 60,595 civilians were killed during the war.

We learned to live with the fear of sudden death, constant scenes of chaos, trailing hoses, puddles of water and debris everywhere in the streets. It was not until November that Churchill confirmed that we were being attacked by rockets, although we had suspected it for some weeks.

The Allied advance was checked by strong German resistance during the winter of 1944-45, delaying final victory by some months. That winter was severe and desolate, dragging on like the war itself. Everyone was depressed and fed up as the V2 raids continued. No wonder there was such a release of emotion and wild rapture when victory finally came.

The German offensive in the Ardennes finally collapsed in January and, as the Russians entered Germany, we could sniff victory in the air. But at home potatoes and coal became very scarce, there were further power cuts, and the queues outside ironmongers' stores for paraffin became longer.

By this time I had completely forgotten what is was like to live in a country at peace. I could not imagine windows without netting or tape, clear peaceful skies, being without fear of death crashing down upon us, shops and streets bright with lights, to see a larder full of unrestricted supplies of food, to have a father living at home, to be able to travel whenever and wherever we wished, to bathe in the sea, to sunbathe on a beach. I tried hard to conceive of such a heaven, but my mind was too limited for the task.

* * *

Council surveyors began to call on all homes, making note of every crack in walls and ceilings before sending in builders to begin the huge task of repairing all war damage free of charge. Hardly a house had escaped.

The little flags on our wall map were moving towards Germany. Russian flags reached Berlin in the spring, the Union Jacks crossed the Rhine in March. Also in March the last V2 fell, on Orpington in Kent. More details were coming to light of concentration camp horrors. Pictures of wasting bodies of the inmates at Belsen were shocking. The long-awaited Russian-American link up took place in April at the River Elbe. The official end of the blackout came in April although people had already become lax.

* * *

Towards the end of the war a very attractive young lady dressed in Canadian Air Force uniform unexpectantly knocked on the door. She introduced herself as Doris, daughter of Richard Hollings, my grandfather's brother who had emigrated to Canada at the turn of the century. Thus I learned that we had cousins in Canada as well as New Zealand. She was stationed at Odiham in Hampshire and looked us up before returning home. I was thrilled when she left me her bicycle. Being old and somewhat rusty it was not easy to ride but I made great use of it. The children in our road formed a cycling club and enjoyed cycling through London to Richmond Park, or north to Stanmore, once the war was over.

* * *

When the danger of invasion had passed, beaches along the coast reopened one by one as the mines were gradually cleared. We made good use of the one beach at Lancing which had been opened during the last months of the war. Before then, we had swum in the River Adur where it winds its way between the lower slopes of the Downs in the shadow of the tall stately Lancing College Chapel, on its way to the sea at Shoreham. That had been fun, but nothing compared to being allowed now to paddle, splash and swim in the sea.

Our delight knew no bounds. Novelty led us to spend every hour of daylight on the beach, leaving only when hunger beckoned. It took just five minutes to walk from sea to bungalow, dripping with seawater, trailing seaweed and leaving sandy footprints in our wake. Nanna prepared picnics for the beach and, being a strong swimmer, often joined us in the water. Sometimes she made an early morning cup of tea for us, only to find our beds empty. We had already left for the beach, returning an hour later for breakfast absolutely ravenous. She called us her water-babies.

We enjoyed venturing further afield, often walking into Worthing one way or Shoreham the other. Our family had always enjoyed seafood such as prawns, winkles, crabs and shrimps, so one day Bronia suggested that we walk along the beach to hunt for shrimps. Nanna was startled when we returned with a bathing cap full of water and shrimps which Bronia had carefully carried home. Nanna boiled them, but after we had watched them trying to jump out of the saucepan in agony, we weren't so keen on eating them.

Gradually the rolls of barbed wire were dismantled and we were able to use the beaches more freely. The enormous concrete blocks remained a while longer allowing children to play on and around them. The gaps between were just too wide to jump over, except for the very daring and agile like Michael. I never attempted it. Those blissful weeks each year at Lancing were among the happiest of our childhood.

While we were spending some of our Easter holiday there, news came through of the death of President Roosevelt. The nation lost a good friend, and we thought how sad it was that he did not live quite long enough to share in the triumph of victory.

7

It's All Over

When they realised all was lost, Hitler and Goebbels committed suicide, their bodies found in Hitler's bunker in Berlin. The official surrender of the German forces followed on 6th May 1945.

Everyone went absolutely wild with happiness, excitement and relief. Church bells rang out for the first time in nearly six years and people danced in the streets with unrestrained joy, even strangers spontaneously hugging each other. Flags and bunting were strung everywhere. May 8th was declared 'VE Day' – Victory in Europe. Street parties were hurriedly organised and one was held in our small cul-de-sac. Bonfires were lit everywhere.

Accompanied by Bronia, her friend Joan and her mother, I visited Trafalgar Square, a mistake I was never to repeat during times of national celebration. The density of the crowd was frightening. We could not move and were crushed against each other. The only way to reach the tube station was to crawl over the bonnets and roofs of cars jammed to a standstill.

The air of carefree gaiety lasted several days. The whole

VE Day celebrations in London, 8th May 1945. Soldiers and girls dance in a street near Berkeley Square. (© Imperial War Museum AP65885)

population was united in its exultant celebrations, like one huge happy family.

After the parties and celebrations were over, a strange thing happened. Suddenly, unbelievably, all the camaraderie, concern for one's neighbour, the caring and sharing, seemingly vanished. Everybody returned home, closed the front door on his own private world and once more assumed the mantle of reticence that is so typically British.

It was all over. People again became strangers. Why does it take a disaster to bring out the inherent goodness of people? We know it lies there under the surface, but we rarely see evidence of it until trouble or tragedy strikes.

Newspaper reports soon reminded us that the war was not yet over in the Far East. Lives were still being lost, battles fought, in the struggle against Japan. It would take the dropping of two atomic bombs to end it, three months later.

It was a long time before life and conditions in the country returned to normal. Food remained scarce and rationing continued. Even five years later bananas were being sold only from under the counter to favourite customers. When Bronia saw her first post-war banana she had to be shown how to peel it.

* * *

Each man returning home from military service was issued with a demob suit, usually badly fitting and of poor quality. After Dad was demobbed he never spoke of the war or his part in it. He casually picked up the threads of his civilian working life in a newspaper office as if the previous six years had never happened. Not for him reminiscences, reunions, or war films ('actors could never portray accurately what we went through'). He drew a curtain across the whole episode.

A corner of the curtain was lifted slightly some years later when Dad boarded a No. 60 bus. He and the conductor stared at each other in disbelief before breaking out in excited greetings and affectionate back-slapping. The bus was held up for five minutes as the two ex-marines looked back on old times and brought knowledge of each other's life up-to-date.

It was difficult for returning servicemen to resume family life after a few years' absence. Our family also experienced some of the problems of re-adjustment we had been warned to expect. For some months Dad tried to run our home as if it were a military camp, having strict rules and making out duty rotas. It nearly drove Mum crazy. On Sundays she was to do nothing. We children were to prepare, cook and clear each meal, and complete other household chores as directed. We all hated and resented it, as Dad scrutinised our every move but did very little himself. We eventually rebelled, even Mum.

Gradually, family life settled down to normal. We were aware how lucky we were to have come through those years of upheaval alive and healthy when so many did not, and we gave thanks.

Jacqueline and Bronia just after the end of the war, summer 1945.

* * *

Because there had been no social life for us for many years, I had few clothes other than a school uniform – the need had never arisen. I did not even own a 'best dress', but it became necessary to expand my wardrobe a little as I grew older. We could not afford new clothes, so for years I wore hand-me-downs from two older girls in our road, and these in turn were passed down to Bronia. Jumble sales proved a useful source of supply. There was a lot of making-do, mending, altering and adjusting for many years, with Mum's sewing machine constantly on the go.

During tube journeys into the City I took an impish delight in joining other passengers in peeling the sticky net off the windows bit by stubborn bit. It seemed strange at first to be able to enjoy an unfettered view of the world through clear windows; very strange.

Not long after the end of the war Michael, then aged about ten, wrote to Montgomery to thank him for looking after his father and was thrilled to receive a signed reply in which Monty sent his 'best wishes for the future to you and your family'.

* * *

My introduction to politics came at school. Ten of us were seated around the dinner table one day, eating the usual unappetising mish-mash, when the older girl supervising us suddenly asked, 'Who are your parents voting for in the election?' The question prompted a spate of excited chatter, but I had no idea what they were talking about.

She repeated the question to each girl in turn, the replies being either Labour or Conservative, but mostly the former. By the time she came to me, a mental eeny-meeny-miny-mo had come up with an answer. Guffaws, jeers, sniggers and scorn greeted my reply of 'Conservative'. Turning a bright red I sank to the very bottom of the imaginary hole I had quickly dug for myself. 'Why?' everyone asked rather aggressively. I could offer no explanation, so my ignorance and embarrassment prompted more laughter.

I asked Dad about it later. Although he held strong views, he tried to give me a fair unbiased appraisal of the two major parties as he saw them. He pointed out that, in times of great national emergency, it was essential that all the main services, fuel supplies, food distribution, industry, farming and the armed forces should come under the rule of Central Government which could organise everything under its control to ensure maximum cooperation, efficiency and united effort, as had been the case during the war. Perhaps also in its aftermath, it would help the country recover and get back on its feet. With this in mind the Labour Party planned to nationalise all the major services and industries, and expand the welfare state which was started in a small way by Liberals earlier in the century. Higher taxation would pay for all this.

The Conservative view was that complete central control was unnecessary in normal peacetime conditions. There was an instinctive dislike of one's life being controlled by bureaucrats in Whitehall. People were happier and better motivated when they had freedom of choice and individual liberty. Wasn't that what we had been fighting for?

Lower taxation meant more money for individuals to invest in small businesses, creating more work to keep men employed. Healthy competition between smaller firms encouraged efficiency and lower prices. Public money should be spent only on those in true need, e.g. the sick, poor, unemployed and old.

I mulled this over for a while and could see common sense in both viewpoints. Why couldn't we combine the best from both parties? Why couldn't we have the best brains from each party to form the government? Dad had

Jacqueline aged 21 in 1952.

no satisfactory answers to my questions, other than the glib, 'Things aren't done that way.'

Despite the hurt I still felt from the rude and scornful young lefties at school, I thought Labour's policies would probably prove best for the first years of peace during the nation's recovery. There was so much to be done, so much clearing up to do, and massive reorganisation as industry reverted to civil from military production. So I was not very surprised when Labour won the first post-war General Election.

Michael aged 18 in 1952.

By nature I felt I leaned towards Conservatism for the long term, but I planned to keep an open mind for the future, to wait and see what life had in store. Only experience could gradually shape a viewpoint one way or the other. It would be interesting to await developments, to discover how we would all progress, nationally and individually.

To quote from a recent broadcast: 'Britain won the war. Now she had to win the Peace.'

Postscript

During the years after the war I continued my music training and, after a brief spell of performing, married and settled down to family life in Bristol, later moving to Kent. I have taught music privately as well as in a wide variety of schools. My family includes one daughter, three sons, eight grandchildren and two great-grandchildren. I still teach piano in West Sussex.

Bronia became a cellist and skilled pianist but chose nursing for her career, training at the Middlesex Hospital. She became a district nurse, midwife and health visitor in Berkshire and north London. Now retired from general nursing, she works privately as a carer for the elderly in need.

On leaving school, Michael became a compositor's apprentice at St Clement's Press before starting his career as a printing consultant in sales management. In addition to running his own business near Reading, Berkshire, he is a keen amateur musician. He also has children and grand-children and is now retired.

Rose (Nanna) lived until 1963, aged eighty-two.
Dorothy (Mum) joined classes in pottery and landscape painting when she was free of family commitments. After

retiring, Stanley (Dad) studied classical music composing at Morley College. Both lived to the age of eighty, until 1987 and 1988 respectively.

Jacqueline Hollings, 2009

Thanks are due to:

The Imperial War Museum for permission to use selected photographs.

Joanna Lecuyer for typing the original manuscript.

Sara Watt for her enthusiasm and setting me on the road to publication.

Michael and Patricia Hollings for their encouragement and support.